CELEBRATING THE FAMILY NAME OF ALVAREZ

Celebrating the Family Name of Alvarez

Walter the Educator

Silent King Books
a WhichHead Entertainment Imprint

First Printing, 2024

Disclaimer

Celebrating the Family Name of Alvarez is a memory book that belongs to the Celebrating Family Name Book Series by Walter the Educator. Collect them all and more books at WaltertheEducator.com

USE THE EXTRA SPACE TO DOCUMENT YOUR FAMILY MEMORIES THROUGHOUT THE YEARS

ALVAREZ

From mountain peaks to oceans wide,

Celebrating the Family Name of

Alvarez

The name of Alvarez beams with pride.

A tapestry rich, woven with care,

A story told through earth and air.

With roots that reach beneath the ground,

Where ancient histories are found,

The Alvarez name, bold and bright,

Guides us forward in the night.

Born of strength and courage rare,

With hearts that know the weight they bear.

The Alvarez walk, with heads held high,

Beneath the sun, beneath the sky.

Their hands have crafted, built with skill,

Through valleys deep, and up the hill.

A family tied by bonds so strong,

A spirit that's endured so long.

Celebrating the Family Name of

Alvarez

In every step, they leave their mark,

A flicker bright within the dark.

The Alvarez hold, in every hand,

The wisdom of this ancient land.

Their voices sing with melodies,

Of winds that dance through olive trees.

Of fields that bloom with endless green,

Where all that's pure and true is seen.

From generation to the next,

The Alvarez write their sacred text.

With love, with honor, they proclaim,

The lasting power of their name.

For every challenge they have faced,

They've moved with courage, filled with grace.

Through every storm, through every fire,

The Alvarez rise, climb even higher.

Their spirit never bends or breaks,

For every step is one that makes

The future bright, the past alive,

In every heartbeat, they survive.

Celebrating the Family Name of

Alvarez

The Alvarez know the value, deep,

Of promises they always keep.

A family built on faith and trust,

On dreams that never turn to dust.

ABOUT THE CREATOR

Walter the Educator is one of the pseudonyms for Walter Anderson. Formally educated in Chemistry, Business, and Education, he is an educator, an author, a diverse entrepreneur, and he is the son of a disabled war veteran. "Walter the Educator" shares his time between educating and creating. He holds interests and owns several creative projects that entertain, enlighten, enhance, and educate, hoping to inspire and motivate you. Follow, find new works, and stay up to date with Walter the Educator™

at WaltertheEducator.com